Games on Horses

Cheryl Case

ISBN: 1537397206
ISBN-13: 978-1537397207

To My Fellow Instructors

Every year I am inspired by you. Every year each of you learn more about how to improve your student riders reminding me that what we do is important. It is validation that we can make a difference, and want to do more. I believe that our students are some of the most talented in the world and it is our job to show them their worth. Through engagement, encouragement and entertainment we can inspire our students to challenge themselves, be happier and dream bigger.

Many of you have requested a list of the games that I play with my students. The truth is that a list won't help you – the games require instructions, diagrams and images.

Let Games on Horses and its supporting website http://www.GamesOnHorses.com serve you in your important work.

Thank you again for everything that you do, that you are and that you create in your arenas.

Cheryl

TABLE OF CONTENTS

Please Note: All information provided in Games on Horses is for general informational purposes only. While we try to keep the information up-to-date and correct, there are no representations or warranties, express or implied, about the completeness, accuracy, reliability, suitability or availability with respect to the information, products, services, or related graphics contained in this hook for any purpose. **Any use of this information is at your own risk.**

Make the Sandwich

The Make the Sandwich game requires the rider to concentrate on a balanced position with good rein use and to sequence the sandwich as shown on the card.

Objective

Follow the specific pattern on the card to make sandwich.

Materials

- Sandwich game pieces
- Game cards

Setup

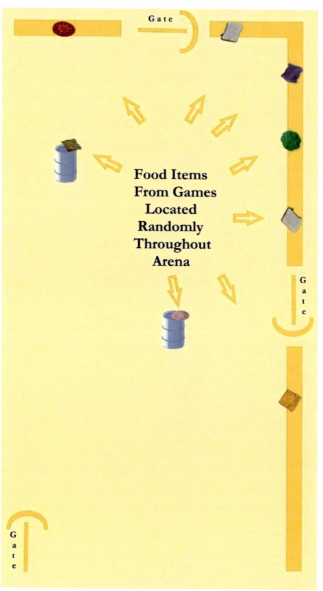

Gate

Food Items
From Games
Located
Randomly
Throughout
Arena

Gate

Gate

(This arena example shows ledges on two sides and three gates.)

- Place all sandwich pieces throughout the arena area.

How to Play

1. Hand one card to each rider.
2. Have each rider guide their horse, stop, line up the horse and pick up a sandwich piece in the order as shown on the card.
3. Ride to the next piece. Repeat until the sandwich is complete.
4. Return the completed sandwich to the instructor to check the pattern.

If time allows, hand out another card and play again.

Riding skills development

You can make your own rules to fit your specific lesson goals. Incorporate the trot, 2-point, walking over poles, walk through a patch made of poles, or any other skill while playing the game. (See relay and obstacle courses on following pages.)

Remember Safety should always be the first concern.

Relay Race

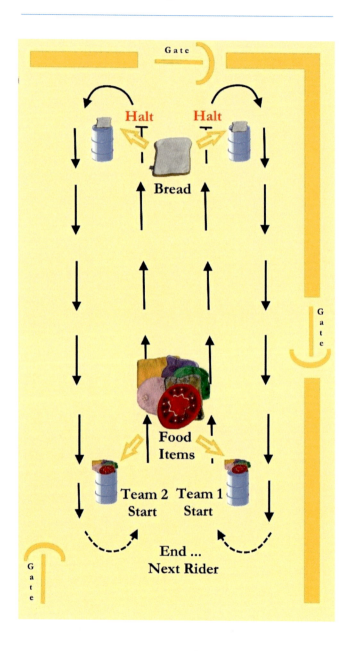

Setup

- Place two sets of the two barrels in a row, equal distance apart. (Four barrels total.)
- Place all food items and one bread slice on one barrel at team start.
- Place a bread slice on the other barrel.

How to Play

1. Rider picks up one food item at a time from the team's start barrel. (Not the bread slice).
2. Ride to second barrel of the set.
3. Place the food item onto the bread (or last food item on the sandwich).
4. Return to first barrel and continue until sandwich complete.

The last piece to go on the sandwich is the bread on top.

First team to build a complete sandwich from all their food items is the winner.

Obstacle Course

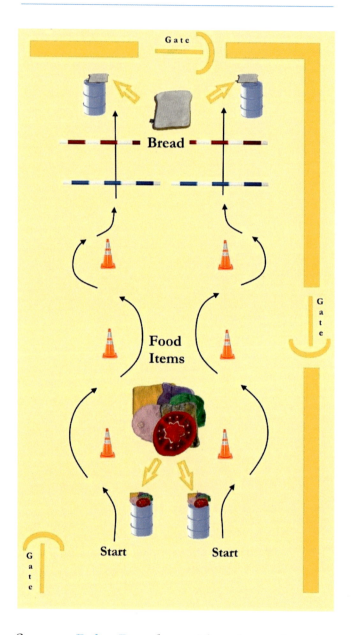

Same as Relay Race but with poles and cones.

Variations

- Set an egg timer – time the activity.
- Call out a number of pieces to find instead of following the card pattern. Each piece must be different. Have the rider count out the number of pieces when done.
- See who can pick up the most pieces and make the tallest sandwich. Have rider count out the number of pieces when done.

Rules were to find six favorite pieces	
Letting the riders work their own imagination likes and dislikes, makes for enjoyment for all.	One rider brought his sandwich back with six pieces of cheese. Another had no tomatoes. She doesn't like tomatoes. Another had three peanut butter pieces and three bread slices. One made a sandwich without bread. A different rider made a sandwich with every piece she could find in the arena to make the tallest sandwich.

Make the Sandwich

Stack The Cake

This game can incorporate any gait depending on the skill level of the riders playing the game. Safety should always be the first concern.

Build the cake by collecting the largest piece [Number 10] first and ending with the top smallest piece [Number 1].

Materials

- 1 Barrel
- Cake piece numbers 1 to 10

For your convenience

Materials, including the Smart Snacks Stack & Count Layer Cake game shown, are available through **GamesOnHorses.com**

9

Setup

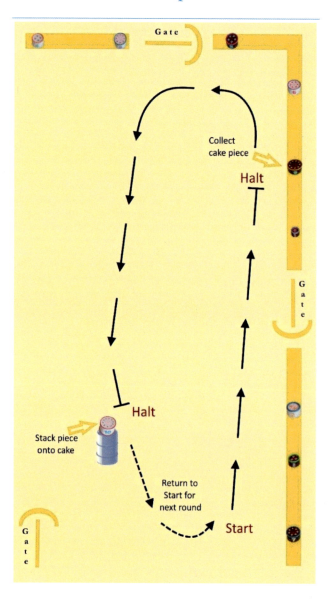

(This arena example shows ledges on two sides and three gates.)

Setup (continued)

- Set barrel in the middle of the arena.
- Place cake pieces randomly throughout the arena.

How to Play

1. Rider rides around the arena to locate the number 10 piece. Rider then halts next to that piece. Rider transfers reins to one hand then stretches to pick up the piece.

2. Rider rides back to the rider's assigned barrel carrying the piece. Rider halts horse next to the barrel. Rider secures reins in one hand then bends and gently places the cake piece onto the barrel.

3. Repeat until all 10 pieces are stacked. (Note: Largest number to smallest.)

Note: If two riders are playing, assign one rider to collect even numbered pieces and the other to rider collects the odd numbered pieces working together to build the cake.

Relay Race

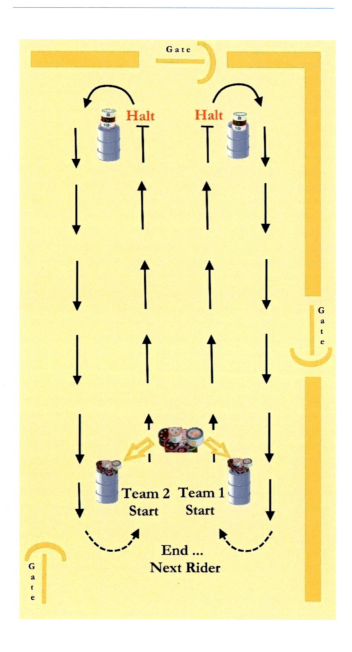

Setup

- Place two sets of two barrels in a row, equal distance apart. (Four barrels total.)
- Place all cake pieces on its own barrel at team start.

How to Play

1. Rider picks up one piece at a time from the team's start barrel.
2. Rider carries piece to rider's assigned second barrel.
3. Build the cake:
   a. The first piece [number 10] goes directly on the barrel).
   b. Subsequent pieces stack on the last layer built.
4. Rider rides back to the first barrel and repeats the process until the cake is complete.

First team to complete their cake is the winner.

Variation using a single cake set.

Setup by placing pieces numbered 1 through 5 on team 1's barrel and pieces 6 through 10 on team 2's barrel.

Play by building a "small" 5-layer cake [numbers 5 to 1] and a "big" 5-layer cake [numbers 10 to 6] instead of the 10-layer cakes above.

Obstacle Course

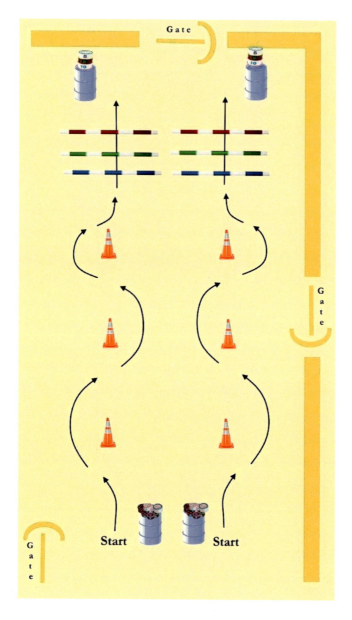

Same as Relay Race but with poles and cones.

Pony Pizza Express

The Pony Pizza Express teaches good rein use by demanding correct steering skill. This game requires good balance to collect and place pizza slices into the box.

Objective

Be the first to build your own pizza and deliver it to the instructor.

Materials

- 2 Barrels
- 2 Pizza Box Games

For your convenience

Materials, including the Melissa & Doug Felt Food Pizza set shown, are available through **GamesOnHorses.com**

Note: The above set comes with all loose pieces. I hot glued all pizza topping pieces together to make it easier to carry.

Setup

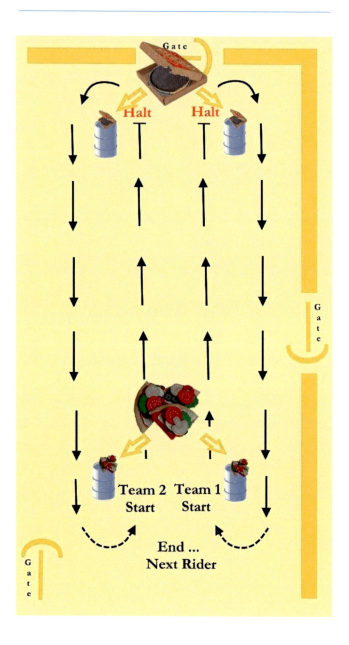

(This arena example shows ledges on two sides and three gates.)

Setup (continued)

- Place barrels in a row with a great deal of space between them.

- One barrel set per rider or team.

- Place all pizza slices on the first barrel.

- Place pizza box with tray inside box on the second barrel.

How to Play

1. Assign a barrel set to each rider or team.

2. Rider halts at first barrel, picks up pizza slice.

3. Rider rides to the second barrel and places the pizza slice into the pizza box correctly.

4. Rider then rides back to the front of the arena.

5. Repeat steps 1 through 4 to complete the pizza.

6. When pizza is complete, rider carries box and delivers it to the instructor.

Obstacle Course

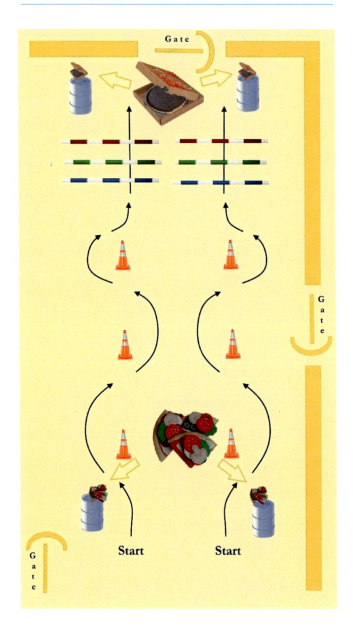

Same as Setup but with poles and cones.

Find the Lost Puppy
(By Name)

The Find the Lost Puppy game incorporates good rein skills, using good balance to line up the horse at the correct location and reading or matching the name of the puppy.

Objective

To find the puppy by matching his name.

Materials

- Stuffed Puppy Toys
- Laminated labels with puppy names[1]
- Game cards with puppy picture (with name tag) on one side and puppy name on the other[2]

---

[1] See How to Make and Attach Labels section at end of this game chapter
[2] See How to Make the Cards section at end of this game chapter

Setup

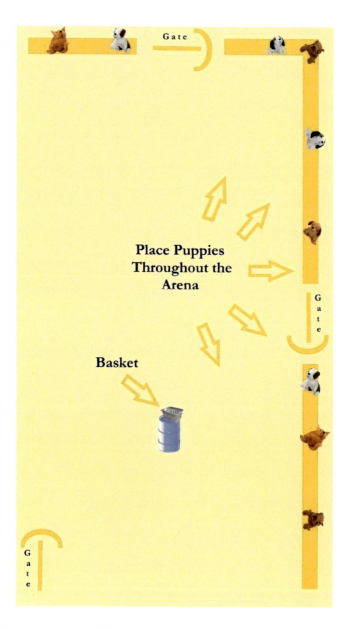

(This arena example shows ledges on two sides and three gates.)

Setup (continued)

- Place all the puppies around the riding arena.

How to Play

1. Hand out four cards to each rider. (Volunteers can carry the cards).

2. Have the rider find the puppy that matches the name on the card.

3. Ride back and place the found puppy into the basket or other container.

4. Repeat until all puppies found.

Variations

- Challenge each rider to ride and pick up all the puppies, one at a time. Count the puppies when done.

- Play the game by color. Find all the black & white puppies.

Relay Race

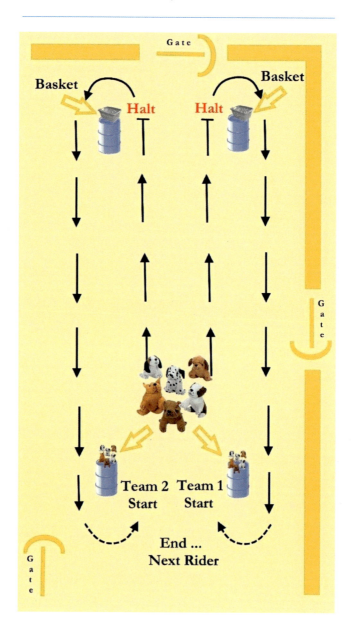

Setup

- Place two sets of two barrels in a row, equal distance apart. (Four barrels total.)
- Place equal number of puppies on each start barrel.

How to Play

1. Pick up one puppy at a time from the team's start barrel.
2. Carry puppy to their second barrel and place into container.
3. Ride back to the first barrel and repeat the process until all puppies are moved to the container.

First team to transport all its puppies is the winner.

Obstacle Course

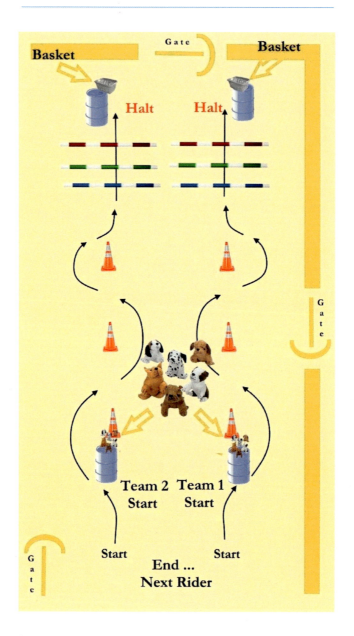

Same as Relay Race but with poles and cones.

How to Make and Attach Name Tags

[Template available at http://www.GamesOnHorses.com]

1. Using text editor (e.g. MS Word, OpenOffice Text, Adobe Acrobat), type and print (½" x 3" more or less) the puppies' names you've chosen.
2. Laminate each page and cut out names.
3. Punch a hole on the left side of the name.
4. Cut covered ponytail hair band.
5. Slide name onto the band and tie around puppy's neck as a collar.

For your convenience
Materials, including puppy toys and prototype name labels, are available through **GamesOnHorses.com**

How to Make the Cards (four to a sheet)

[Template available at http://www.GamesOnHorses.com]

1. Divide the page into four equal quadrants.
   a. For word processing software, insert a 2x2 table and adjust to page size (including default margins).
   b. For spreadsheet software, adjust a1, a2, b1, b2 cells to page size.
   c. You may wish to include borders to simplify trimming in next step.
2. Center a puppy name into each quadrant. Laminate and cut.

HINT: Make just one sheet first (with four items). To make sure that the puppy name and its picture end up on the same card. It is very easy to get them flipped.

On our printer, the pages need to be set up this way:

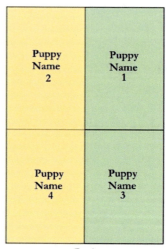

	Front		Back

Front: Puppy Picture 1, Puppy Picture 2, Puppy Picture 3, Puppy Picture 4

Back: Puppy Name 2, Puppy Name 1, Puppy Name 4, Puppy Name 3

Block Balancing

The block balancing game promotes good balance and fine and gross motor skills while having a great time!

Objective

Build a sculpture using blocks shown on card.

Required Materials

- Barrels

- Colored discs

- Colored blocks[3]

- Game cards

For your convenience
Materials, including the Melissa & Doug Block Balancing game shown, are available through **GamesOnHorses.com**

---

[3] The Learning Resources *Blox 360 -3D* set also works well.

Setup

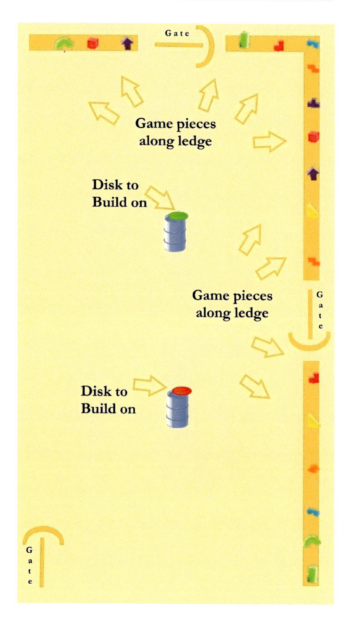

(This arena example shows ledges on two sides and three gates.)

Setup (continued)

- One barrel per rider or team.

- Widely space the two barrels in the middle of the arena -- leave enough room for the rider to safely ride back and forth to collect and build blocks on the colored disc at the assigned barrel.

- Place one colored disc on each barrel (This makes a flat surface to build the blocks and gives the rider a visual clue of which barrel is his or hers.

- Place the building blocks randomly throughout the riding area.

How to Play

1. Assign a barrel with a specific colored disc to each rider (or team).
2. Hand out 4-5 cards to each rider.
3. Have each rider ride to locate the specific block that is pictured on the first card.
4. Halt next to the game piece and pick it up to carry.
5. Ride back to the assigned barrel and place the game piece on the colored disc.
6. Continue to ride, locate and collect each piece, building one on top of the other, until rider has found them all and the structure is complete.

When everyone is finished collecting and building	
The riders love recognition of a job well done	**Take a victory lap to admire everyone's block sculpture.** Recognize the riders by congratulating the one with the 1. Tallest 2. Shortest 3. Widest Use any categories that will fit the activity for your group.

Riding skills development

You can also incorporate additional riding skills while playing the game. Examples include:

- Circle the barrel before rider places the game piece.

- Walk over poles on the way back to the assigned barrel, reminding them "Heels down, eyes up.".

- Use any safe and appropriate skills according to rider's riding abilities.

Relay Race

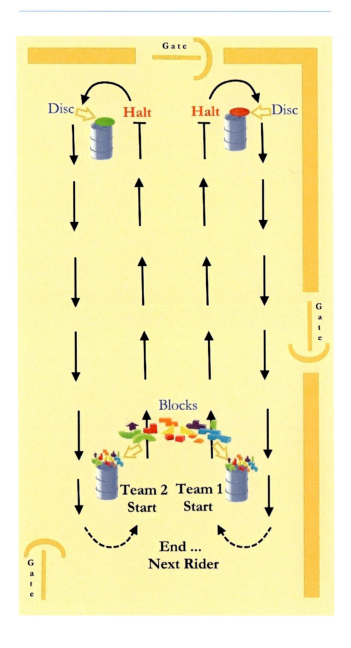

Block Balancing Relay Layout

Setup

- Place two sets of the two barrels in a row, equal distance apart. (Four barrels total.)
- Place all game pieces on one barrel of the set.
- No game cards needed.

How to Play

1. Pick up one block at a time from the team's start barrel.
2. Ride to second barrel of the set.
3. Place block and build one on top of the other.
4. Return to first barrel and continue until all blocks are collected and built.

First team to use all pieces on their barrel to build sculpture is the winner.

Block Balancing

Horse Equipment

This is an excellent learning game about equipment and care of the horse.

Objective

Each rider must decide if the item on the card is used for grooming the horse or a piece of equipment used on the horse. Grooming items go into the grooming box. Items used on the horse go into the basket (or box).

Materials

---

2 Barrels	Halter
Grooming Box	Stirrup
Box or Basket	Leathers
Game Cards	Curry Comb
Mane Brush	Sweat Scraper
English Girth	Soft Brush
Hard Brush	Reins
...(Dandy)	Grooming
Lead Rope	Mitt
Stirrup	Saddle Pad
Shedding Blade	Fly Spray
Hoof Pick	Towel

Note: You do not need all these items. Use as many as you want or have available.

Also, in lieu of the game cards, you can glue pictures from a catalog and write on index cards.

Setup

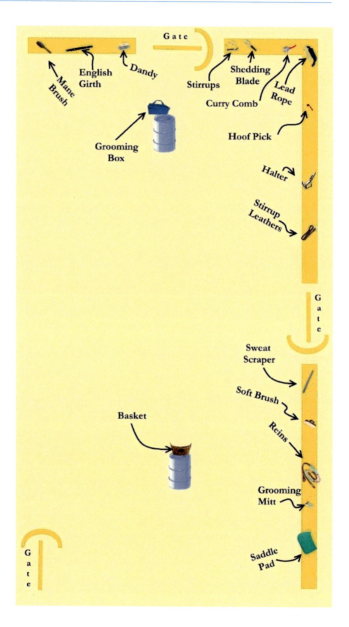

(This arena example shows ledges on two sides and three gates.)

Setup (continued)

- Widely separate two barrels in middle of arena.
- Set grooming box on one barrel.
- Set a basket or box on other barrel.
- Place all barn items randomly throughout the arena.

How to Play

1. Hand out an equal number of random cards to each rider.
2. Have each rider find the item on their first card. Rider must then decide if the item belongs in the grooming box or if it is a piece of equipment that belongs to the horse.
3. Ride to the appropriate location for the item and place the item into the container.
4. Ride and locate the item on the next card and repeat the process.
5. Each rider finds all items on the cards they are given.

At the end, all riders ride to grooming box and talk about each item that was found and how it is used. Go to the other basket and discuss how each item is used on the horse.

Riding skills development

This game teaches riders that there is a lot of time and equipment needed to take care of and prepare the horse to ride. Remember to talk about taking care of the horse after the ride is over, the cool-out process and grooming the horse again before the horse goes back to his stall.

How to Make the Cards (four to a sheet)
[Template available at GamesOnHorses.com]

1. Divide the page into four equal quadrants.
   a. For word processing software, insert a 2x2 table. Adjust to page size (including margins).
   b. For spreadsheet software, adjust a1, a2, b1, b2 cells to page size.
   c. You may wish to include borders to simplify trimming in next step.
2. Center the item name on one side, its picture on the other.
3. Laminate and cut.

HINT: Make just one sheet first (with four items). To make sure that the item and its picture end up on the same card. It is very easy to get them flipped.

On our printer, the pages need to be set up this way:

Equipment Name 1	Equipment Name 3		Equipment Picture 3	Equipment Picture 1
Equipment Name 2	Equipment Name 4		Equipment Picture 4	Equipment Picture 2
For Front			For Back	

Do the Laundry

Do the Laundry game promotes good rein use, balance, correct spacing of horses and following directions to execute each skill.

Objective

Match up pairs of socks and put them in the washing machine.

Materials

- Washing Machine[4]

- Laundry Basket

- 8 to 10 pairs of children's socks

- *Optional*: Wooden Clothes Pins

For your convenience

Materials, including the Melissa & Doug Let's Play House Wash Dry & Iron game shown, are available through **GamesOnHorses.com**

---

[4] For the washing machine you can substitute a box, bucket, basket or whatever you have available.

Setup

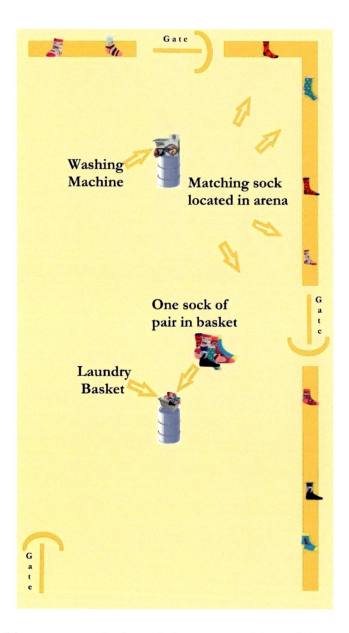

(This arena example shows ledges on two sides and three gates.)

Setup (continued)

- Place one of each pair of socks into laundry basket.
- Place the other remaining socks throughout the riding arena.
- Widely separate two barrels in middle of arena.
- Place washing machine on one barrel.
- Place laundry basket on other barrel.

How to Play

1. Ride to the laundry basket and take out one sock.
2. Ride to find the matching sock for the washing machine.
3. Halt at located sock.
4. Ride carrying pair of socks (or clothes pin them to the horses mane) to the washing machine.
5. Place into the machine.
6. Ride back to the laundry basket.

Repeat until all socks matched and put into washing machine.

Relay

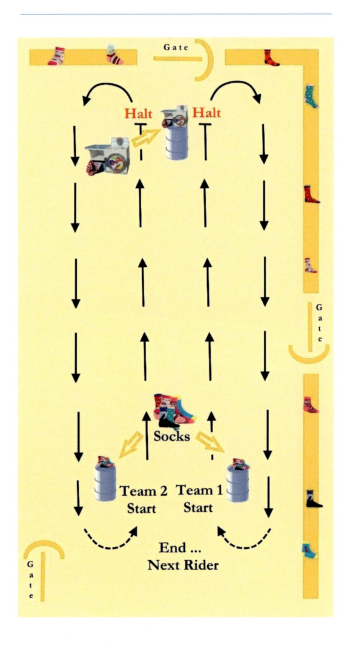

Setup

- Place two barrels in a row, equal distance apart. Place remaining barrel at opposite end of arena. (Three barrels total.)
- Separate the socks into two groups of unmatched socks. That is, there are no matching pairs in the group.
- Place all the (unmatched) socks around the arena.
- Divide the remaining socks equally between the starting barrels
- Place the Washing Machine (or box) on the other barrel.

How to Play

1. Pick up one sock at a time from the team's start barrel.
2. Find the matching sock in the arena.
3. Ride to second barrel that has the washing machine or box.
4. Place the sock pair into the washing machine.
5. Return to first barrel and continue until all sock pairs are in the washing machine.

First team to put all socks from their barrel into the washing machine is the winner.

Obstacle Course

Similar to Relay but with additional barrel, poles and cones.

Advanced Obstacle Course

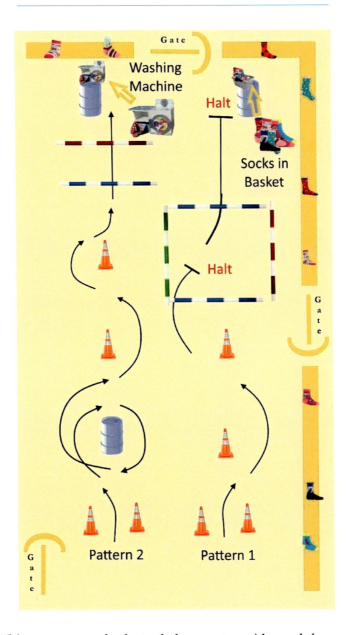

(This arena example shows ledges on two sides and three gates.)

Setup

- Pattern 1
    - o Set two cones as starting gate.
    - o Place two cones in path to steer around.
    - o Layout four poles to create a closed square.
    - o Set basket on a barrel at the end of the arena containing unmatched socks.
    - o Place the other remaining socks of pair throughout the riding arena.
- Pattern 2
    - o Set two cones as starting gate.
    - o Place one barrel in path to circle around.
    - o Layout two cones in path to steer around.
    - o Place two poles in parallel to walk over.
    - o Set washing machine or box on a barrel.

How to Play

1. Ride through the cones in pattern 1 into the closed square and halt.
2. Proceed to laundry basket, halt, take out one sock.
3. Ride to find the matching sock in arena and clothes pin pair to horse's mane.
4. Ride to pattern 2 start position.
5. Circle the Barrel, weave cones and step over poles.
6. Place matched socks in washing machine or box.
7. Ride back to the pattern 1 start.

Repeat until all socks matched and put into washing machine.

Tic Tac Toe

The Tic Tac Toe game encourages good rein use, positioning the horse at the ring, halting skill and strategic planning.

Objective

Place 3 matching game pieces in a row on the pattern.

Materials

- 9 plastic colored rings

- 5 game X-shaped pieces[5]

- 5 game O-shaped pieces

For your convenience
Materials are available through **GamesOnHorses.com**

---

[5] See "How to Make Game Pieces" on last page of this game description

Setup

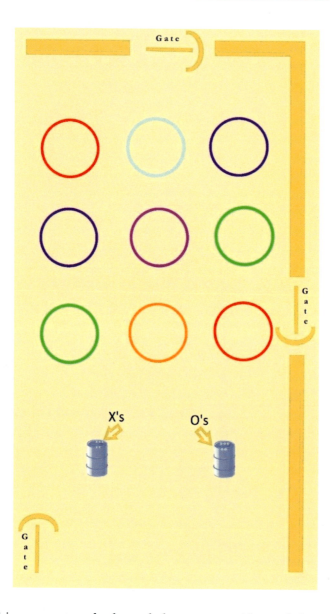

(This arena example shows ledges on two sides and three gates.)

- Place the 9 rings on the ground in traditional Tic-Tac-Toe pattern.

Leave enough space for the horses to fit among hoops.

No stepping on hoops.

Be sure to **emphasize** to your riders and volunteers that the hoops and game pieces are plastic. They may break if stepped on.

- Place 5 X pieces on one barrel, the 5 O pieces on another.
- Assign one rider (or a team of riders) to one of the barrels.
- Assign the other rider (or team) to other barrel.

How to Play

---

1. One rider from each assigned barrel rides and tosses one of their game pieces into one of the rings. That rider comes back to the assigned barrel and waits for their next turn.

2. The next rider takes a turn to ride and toss game piece into the ring.

3. Game continues until a rider or a team gets three in a row or diagonal (in any direction) on the ring pattern. (Three of the same game piece in a row wins.)

Variations

- Toss all game pieces into the pattern. Count the pieces at the end.
- Call out a specific color and have rider toss game piece into that colored ring.
- Have the rider call out a color, ride and toss game piece into that colored ring.
- Use as a relay. See which rider or team can fill the rings up first with their game pieces.

All in Good fun	
Cheating was the Name of the game	The game was made up of four riders, two girls and two boys. Girls against the boys turned ugly. Cheating was the name of the game. It was getting very competitive. Boys were losing every game. The girls' team was more strategic. The boys thought to hide an extra game piece and toss two of them at their turn in order to win quickly. Girls team pointed out it was too bad that the only way to win against them was to cheat. Girls told them their riding skills and strategy to play the game were better. Everyone was laughing and having a great time, while learning to ride their horse through the game.

How to Make Game Pieces

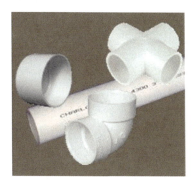

- ½" pvc pipe cut to 3 3/8" lengths.
- ½" pvc caps
- ½" pvc cross fittings
- ½" pvc elbows

There is NO need to GLUE or CEMENT the pieces. This allows easy and quick replacement if any of the pipes break.[6]

FOR 's

Each X requires
- four 3 3/8" pipes
- one cross fitting
- four caps

Insert one end of each pipe into one side of the cross. Place a cap on the other end of the pipe.

FOR 's

Each O requires
- four 3 3/8" pipes
- four elbows

Insert each end of a pipe into elbows to make a square.

---

[6] Though pieces have neither broken nor separated in our experience.

Tic Tac Toe

Red Light / Green Light

Red Light / Green Light teaches riders to use good riding skills to perform each task. It makes riders concentrate to remember what skill goes to each paddle.

Objective

Execute riding skill for the paddle shown.

Materials

- Colored plastic ping pong paddles

For your convenience

Materials, including Spectrum Table Tennis Paddle Set shown, are available through **GamesOnHorses.com**

Setup

(This arena example shows ledges on two sides and three gates.)

Setup (continued)

- Decide what riding skills should go with each colored paddle. For example:

Red: Stop
Green: Walk on
Yellow: Circle right
Purple: Trot
Blue: Back up three steps
Orange: Laugh out loud

How to Play.

1. Leader stands in middle of arena holding up a colored paddle one at a time.
2. While holding up the paddle, leader says the color. Each rider performs the skill that goes with the colored paddle.

Variations

- Use no words. Just hold up the colored paddle.
- Let the riders decide what task goes with each paddle.
- Change the task that goes with each paddle encouraging riders to pay close attention to the activity.
- Let a rider run the game.

Red Light / Green Light

Put the Puppy to Bed

The Put the Puppy to Bed game uses good rein skills and keeping correct spacing while finding the puppy's bed. The game also works on reading skills (or matching skills if pictures are used) to locate the correct bed.

Objective

Put each puppy to bed in his own bed.

Materials

- 10 or more stuffed puppies with name tags[7]
- 1 large basket
- The same number of "beds" as the number of puppies

"Beds" are paper hot dog trays with puppy's name on them.

---

[7] See Page 25 for how to make name tags

Setup

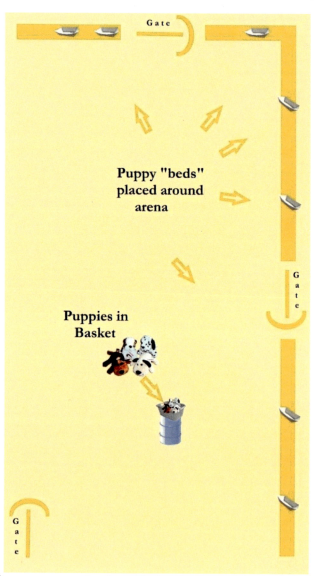

Puppy "beds" placed around arena

Puppies in Basket

Gate

Gate

Gate

(This arena example shows ledges on two sides and three gates.)

- Place beds throughout the riding arena

How to Play

1. Each rider chooses a puppy from the basket and reads the puppy's name.

2. Rider locates the puppy's bed, stops and places puppy into his bed.

3. Continue riding back to basket to retrieve another puppy to put into his bed until all puppies are put to bed.

Variations

- Wake the puppy up. Ride to a puppy in his bed and bring him to the basket.

- Use pictures of puppies instead of names to find in their bed and bring back to a basket.

- After all the puppies are put to bed, hand out washcloths and instruct each rider to stop and reach to cover up each puppy.

Hokey Pokey

The Hokey Pokey promotes rider's listening skills to follow the instructor's directions as well as to develop rein use and balance.

♪ How to Play ♫

♫ *Foot remains in stirrup*	♫ *Foot remains in stirrup*
You put your right foot in	You put your left foot in
You take your right foot out	You take your left foot out
You put your right foot in	You put your left foot in
And you shake it all about	And you shake it all about
You do the hokey pokey	You do the hokey pokey
And you turn your HORSE around	And you turn your HORSE around
That's what it's all about	That's what it's all about
♪ *Hold reins in LEFT hand*	♪ *Hold reins in RIGHT hand*
You put your right hand in	You put your left hand in
You take your right hand out	You take your left hand out
You put your right hand in	You put your left hand in
And you shake it all about	And you shake it all about
You do the hokey pokey	You do the hokey pokey
And you turn your HORSE around	And you turn your HORSE around
That's what it's all about	That's what it's all about

♫ You put your whole HORSE in
♪ You take your whole HORSE out
♫ You put your whole HORSE in
♪ And you shake it all about
♫ You do the hokey pokey
♪ And you turn your HORSE around
That's what it's all about

Make a Snake-lace

Make a Snake-lace works on having good rein use, halting, making horse stop and wait while stretching to retrieve the snake. Balance is necessary to teach better position on the horse.

Objective

Make the specified colored pattern of snakes on horse's neck.

Materials

- 2 Barrels
- 2 Baskets
- 12 or more Stuffed Snake Toys

- Pattern Cards (Laminated cards are optional. You can write color patterns on index cards).

For your convenience, materials including
- Plush Bright Snakes,
- Software to generate random, unique pattern cards and/or card sets
available at GamesOnHorses.com

Setup

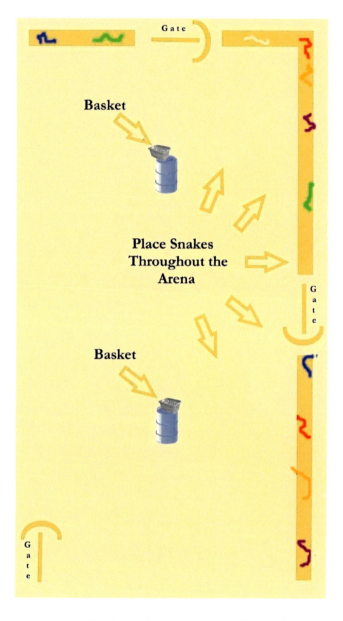

(This arena example shows ledges on two sides and three gates.)

Setup (continued)

- Place all the colored snakes throughout the riding area

- Widely space 2 barrels in the middle of arena

- Place a basket on each barrel

How to Play

1. Assign a barrel to each rider.

2. Hand out cards with a specified pattern.

3. Rider is to locate a specific snake, stop, reach to pick up snake and place it on the horse's neck as a necklace.

4. Ride to the next snake listed on the card and place on the horse's neck.

5. Continue locating each colored snake on the rider's list.

6. When list is complete, ride to a barrel with basket. Read off color list as rider places each snake into the basket.

That round is now complete.

Variations

- In lieu of the cards, call out pattern for the rider to find. (Have the rider say the color pattern when done.)

- Call out a number. Have riders find that number of snakes. Each snake must be a different color.

- See which rider can find most snakes in a timed event.

- Roll dice. Have rider find that number of snakes.

- See which horse's neck can fit the most snakes.

Relay Race

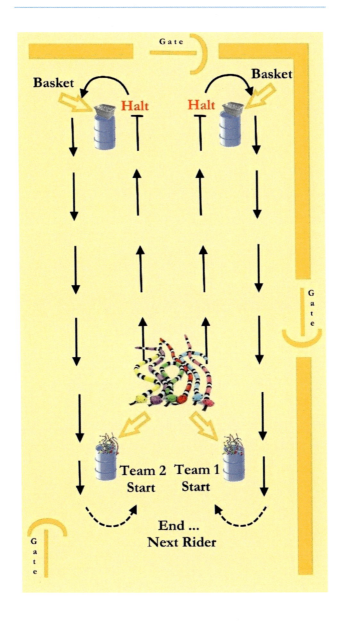

Setup[8]

- Place two sets of the two barrels in a row, equal distance apart. (Four barrels total.)
- Place an equal number of snakes on each barrel on one set of barrels at team start.
- Place a container on each of the remaining two barrels.

How to Play

1. Pick up a snake from the first barrel.
2. Carry snake on horse's neck to the second barrel.
3. Place snake into container.
4. Ride back to the first barrel and repeat the process until all snakes are moved into the container.

First team to move all their snakes into the second container is the winner.

---

[8] Layout shown assumes you chose to get a snake set for each team. As an alternative, you may wish to divide up the pieces from the one set.

Obstacle Course

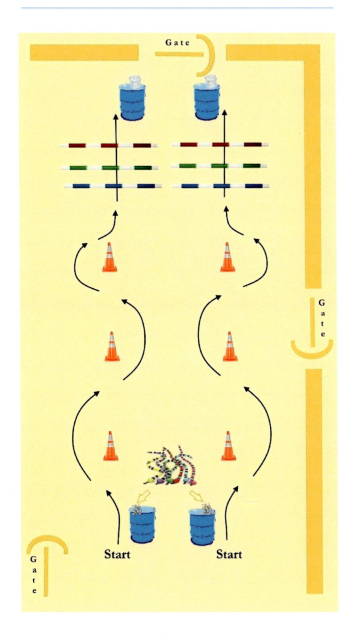

Same as Relay Race but with poles and cones.

Dessert Tray

The Dessert Tray game incorporates gross and fine motor skills with good balance and demands a level of patience to locate and place piece in the correct puzzle slot in the tray.

Objective

Fill the dessert tray with all available pieces.

Materials

- Barrel
- Dessert Tray
- Cookie Pieces
- Cake Pieces

Materials, including the Melissa & Doug Sweet Treat Tower Play set game shown, are available through **GamesOnHorses.com**

Setup

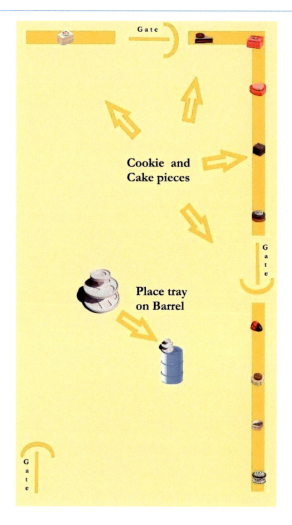

(This arena example shows ledges on two sides and three gates.)

Setup (continued)

- Place barrel in the middle of the arena.
- Set all cookie and cake pieces randomly throughout the riding arena.
- Place tray on barrel.

How to Play

1. Have each rider locate one dessert piece at a time.
2. Pick up the piece and ride back to the other barrel and place piece on the tray in its correct space.
3. Ride to locate the next piece and repeat the process.

Game is over when tray is filled.

Skill development

The Dessert Tray game promotes balance, good rein use, fine and gross motor skills and patience to fit the piece into its correct space.

This game is also a puzzle. Rider must figure out the specific, unique place each piece will fit into the tray.

Relay using a tray set for each team

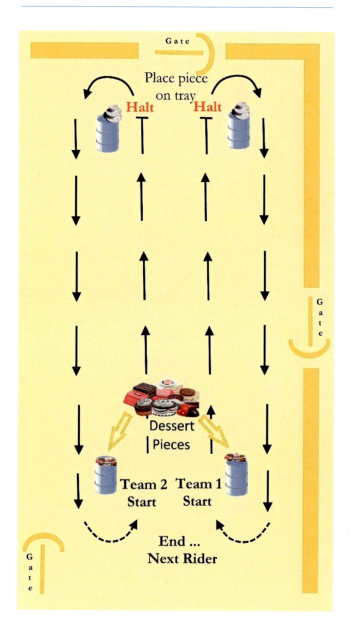

Dessert Tray Relay Layout

Materials

- 2 Desset Sets
- 4 Barrels

Setup

- Place two sets of the two barrels in a row, equal distance apart. (Four barrels total.)
- Place the dessert pieces from each tray set on its own barrel at team start.
- Place the dessert tray on each of the remaining barrels.

How to Play

1. Collect dessert piece from the team's first barrel.
2. Ride to their second barrel carrying the piece.
3. Fit piece into correct space on the cake tray.
4. Ride back to the first barrel and repeat the process until all pieces are placed on the tray.

First team to find and place all pieces in their tray is the winner.

Relay using just one tray set

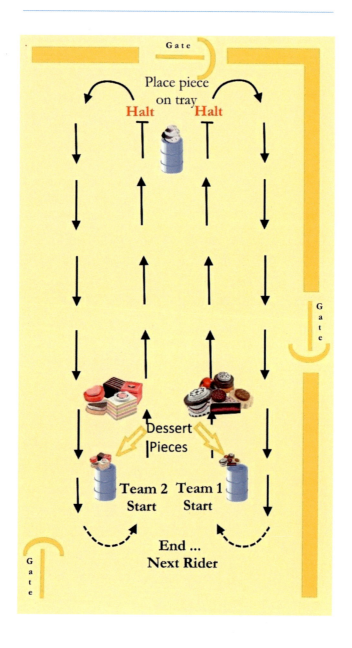

Materials

- 1 Desset Set
- 3 Barrels

Setup

- Place the empty tray on a single barrel at one end of the arena.
- Place two barrels at team start.
- Place an equal number of dessert pieces on each barrel at team start.

How to Play

1. Collect dessert piece from the team's first barrel.
2. Ride to their second barrel carrying the piece.
3. Fit piece into correct space on their tray.
4. Ride back to their first barrel and repeat the process until all pieces are placed on the tray.

First team to find and place all their team's pieces in the tray is the winner.

Obstacle Course

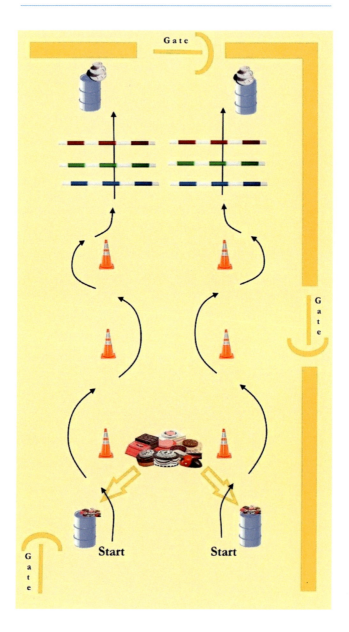

Similar to Relay but with additional barrel, poles and cones.

Water Bottle Race

The Water Bottle game promotes good steering skills with good balance to carry and hand off the bottle to the next rider.

Objective

Ride the pattern and place all assigned bottles into the container at the end of the pattern.

Materials

- 4 barrels
- 3 to 5 small (8 oz.) water bottles per rider. (May mark each bottle with colored tape to designate teams.)
- A bucket or container to hold the water bottles
- Poles, Barrels and Cones for arena

Setup

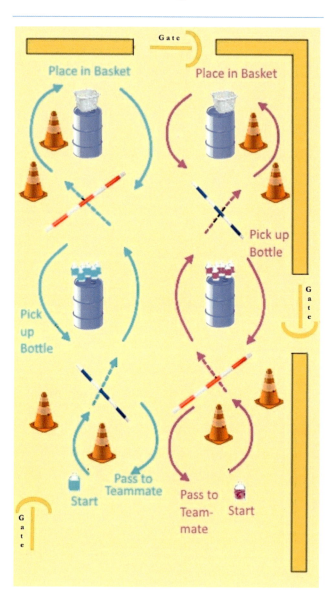

(This arena example shows ledges on two sides and three gates.)

How to Play

1. Each rider starts out carrying a small bottle of water.
2. Ride through the pattern and place bottle into a bucket.
3. Finish riding through the pattern, stop to pick up another bottle and ride to hand it off to your partner.
4. Each team continues through the pattern until all their bottles are in the bucket.

Variations

- Set an egg timer. Winner has the most bottles in bucket in designated time.
- Tape each bottle in different colored tape and use as a color match game. Have each rider pick up a specific color.

Zoo Animals

Zoo Animals promotes good rein use, gross and fine motor skills and promotes concentration to recall animal facts at game's end.

Objective

For each card, collect the specific animal then ride to the next location and place into basket.

Materials

- 2 Barrels
- Toy animals
- Pictures of the animals (or from the Internet) that match your toy animals.
- Facts about animals are on the back of each card.[9] [See facing page for examples.]

For your convenience
Materials are available through **GamesOnHorses.com**

---

[9] See How to Make Cards section at end of this game chapter.

Setup

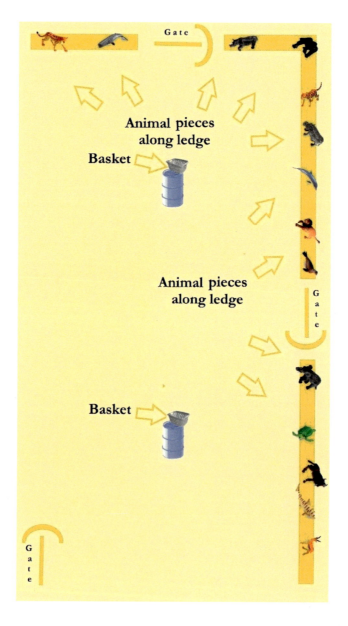

Animal pieces along ledge

Basket

Animal pieces along ledge

Basket

Gate

Gate

Gate

- Place toy animals throughout the riding area.

How to Play

1. Hand out four to five cards to each rider.
2. Assign a barrel with a basket on it for rider to place retrieved animal.
3. Have each rider locate the matching animal, halt, line up the horse and pick up the toy.
4. Carry the animal toy and ride back to assigned barrel and place animal into the basket.
5. Repeat the task until rider finds all of their animals.

Skills development

- Make sure to read the information from the back of each card throughout the game.
- When all animals have been found, ask a question from the cards. For example "Who found the fastest large cat? How fast can it run?" "What is the largest bear?"

Variations

- Set an egg-timer. Time the activity.
- Call out characteristic of specific animal and have rider find that animal (e.g. "Lives in water. The baby is called a calf.").

Relay Race

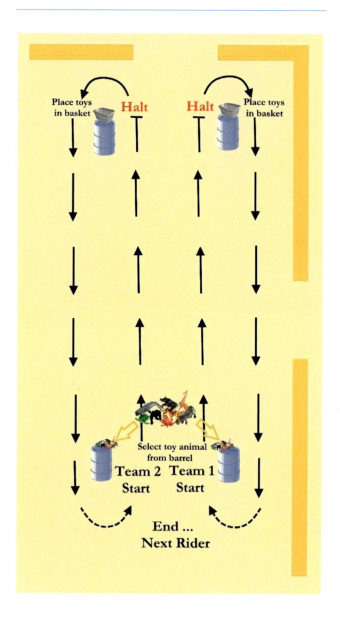

Materials

- 4 Barrels
- Toy animals
- No cards needed.

Setup

- Place two sets of two barrels in a row, equal distance apart. (Four barrels total.)
- Place equal number of toy animals on each start barrel.

How to Play

1. Pick up one toy animal at a time from the team's start barrel.
2. Carry toy to team's second barrel.
3. Place the toy animal in the basket
4. Ride back to the first barrel and repeat the process until the all animals in basket.

First team to transport all animals is the winner.

Obstacle Course

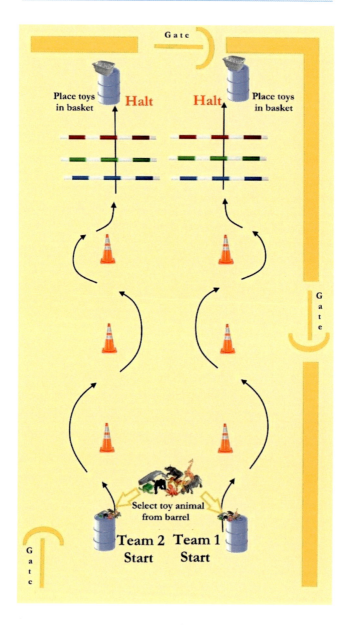

Same as Relay Race but with poles and cones.

How to Make the Cards (four to a sheet)

Divide the page into four equal quadrants.
  a. For word processing software, insert a 2x2 table and adjust to page size (including default margins).
  b. For spreadsheet software, adjust a1, a2, b1, b2 cells to page size.
  c. You may wish to include borders to simplify trimming in next step.
Center animal picture on one side, its facts on the other. Laminate and cut.

HINT: Make just one sheet first (with four animals). Make sure that the animal picture and its facts end up on the same card. It is very easy to get them flipped.

On our printer, the pages need to be set up this way:

Animal Picture 1	Animal Picture 2		Animal Fact 2	Animal Fact 1
Animal Picture 3	Animal Picture 4		Animal Fact 4	Animal Fact 3
For Front			For Back	

[Templates available at GamesOnHorses.com]

Lucky Duck

The Lucky Duck game teaches balance, coordination, working with fine and gross motor skills and counting.

Objective

Move all ducks to the last container.

Materials

- (20 to 30) plastic or rubber ducks
- Six barrels
- single die (dice)
- two large bowls or buckets
- Nets with a short handle (One for each rider)

For your convenience
Materials are available through **GamesOnHorses.com**

Note: The game pieces are also easy to clean. Wipe off the ducks and dice with a damp cloth and the nets wash nicely with a little soap and water.

Setup

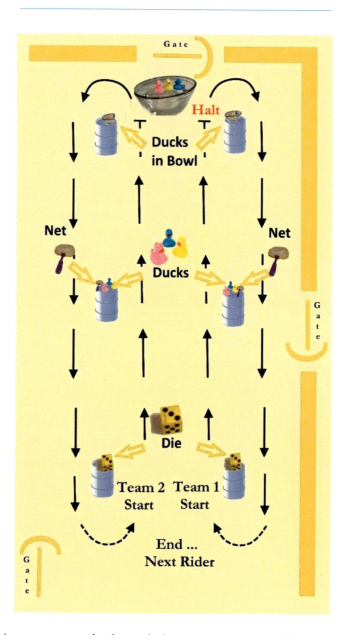

(This arena example shows ledges on two sides and three gates.)

- Line up the three barrels equal distant from each other in a row down one side of the arena. Repeat the same on the other side of riding area.
- First barrel has one die (dice) on it.
- Second barrel contains all the ducks and a net.
- Third barrel has empty container such as a bowl.

How to Play

1. Play this game with one or two riders or teams.
2. Rider or first team player rides to first barrel, halts and rolls the die (keep the die on the barrel). *Remember the number rider rolled.*
3. Ride to the second barrel. Rider halts, picks up net and scoops the number of ducks that rider rolled on the die.
4. Ride to the last barrel carrying the ducks in the net. Halt and put the ducks into the bowl. (Rider now can carry the net throughout the ride or have a volunteer carry it.)
5. Ride back to the front and repeat the sequence until all the ducks are moved to the last container.
6. The riders on the other side of the arena do the same. The first rider or team to move all their ducks to the last container wins.

Riding skills development

Any gait or skill can be incorporated to ride back to the front such as Walk, Trot, Canter, Weave cones, 2-point..

Keep in mind, use safety and appropriate skills for the rider's level of riding.

Obstacle Course

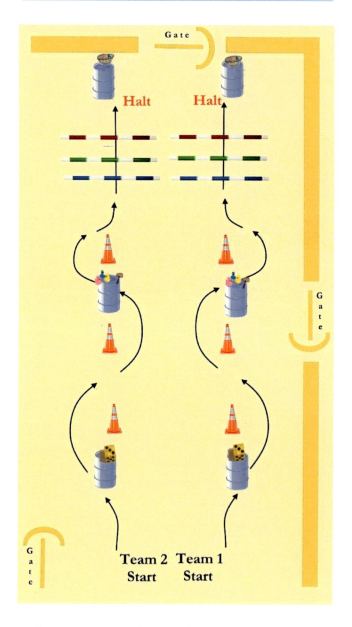

Same as Setup but with poles and cones.

About the Author

Upon Cheryl Case's receipt of the *American Association of Mental Retardation* Award in 2006, Illinois United States Senator Dick Durban officially recognized Cheryl into the Congressional Record for her outstanding efforts to enrich the lives of people with developmental disabilities in Illinois.

Cheryl, a Path International Association Advanced Instructor, gained her certification upon graduation from Equest's N.A.R.H.A. Therapeutic Riding Instructor Training Program. She also earned continuing education units through *Texas A&M University*. She has served as a Special Olympic coach since 2003 and previously owned and operated her own Therapeutic center.

Today Cheryl teaches and coaches Special Olympics at a PATH Premier Accredited Therapeutic Center in Illinois continuing a life-long love of owning and showing horses and of instructing riders for over 30 years.

Made in the USA
Columbia, SC
10 June 2021